ROLLS-ROYCE

– the first cars from Crewe

Ken Lea

HISTORICAL SERIES No 23

Published in 1997 by the
Rolls-Royce Heritage Trust
P O Box 31 Derby England

ISBN: 1 872922 10 4

The Historical Series is published as a joint initiative by the Rolls-Royce Heritage Trust and The Sir Henry Royce Memorial Foundation.

Previous volumes published in the series are listed at the rear.

Cover: MarkVI Bentley standard steel saloon.

Books are available from:
Rolls-Royce Heritage Trust, Rolls-Royce plc, Moor Lane, PO Box 31, Derby DE24 8BJ

Origination and Reproduction by Neartone Ltd, Arnold, Nottingham
Printed by Premier Print, Glaisdale Parkway, Bilborough, Nottingham

DEDICATION

Just before this book was to be passed to the printers for publication, I was greatly saddened to learn that Alec Harvey-Bailey had died on the evening of 3 March 1997. Alec's contribution to the fortunes of Rolls-Royce was far reaching and in later years centred on aero-engines. However, he never lost his interest in cars and in particular had a keen sense of what was the ethos of Rolls-Royce and Bentley. Given other circumstances, he would undoubtedly have taken on his father's developments a lot further. With his passing, we have lost one of the first-hand links with the pre-war era. His brilliant recall has illuminated many of the decisions taken by the figures of the time within the Company and fortunately he has put many of them onto paper. I counted him amongst my greatest friends and, at difficult times, he was a true mentor. Therefore, I dedicate this book, which would not have been written without his help and encouragement, to Alec Harvey-Bailey and to his wife Joan who was his constant companion and to whom he was clearly devoted.

K E Lea
March 1997

CONTENTS

FOREWORD

When I was a much younger man and was working for the Company in the thirties, I had the good fortune to be able to drive the products of the Chassis Division which was, at that time, led by my father. He was rather a reserved character not given to voicing strong opinions in open forum but quite capable of saying to senior engineering colleagues, when the inevitable failure occurred, that they had been warned! What was hidden from public gaze was a strong and determined character who had great perception and one who made his influence properly felt in private.

It is my view that this narrative, written by Ken Lea, has given a true and revealing insight into the views of various senior figures in the Company during the period 1936 to 1954, but he has also captured the political influences of the time with real clarity. It is against this background that one must view the pre-war engineering programmes and their subsequent effect on the first models of cars that were produced from the Company's factory at Crewe from 1946.

I have no hesitation in endorsing Ken Lea's comments and I also must add particularly that the eight-cylinder B-range-engined cars that were in the experimental fleet at the outbreak of the Second World War showed significant promise. Given other events, one can easily surmise that their impact on the Company's customers would have been both beneficial and profound. Another car that sticks in my memory was an experimental Bentley of the same period and which was chassis 3-B-50. When eventually fitted with what was to become the engine for the Mk VI Bentley and a low-loss dual exhaust, I remember, so well, how lively was the performance which perfectly matched the ride and handling.

Following the outbreak of war, my own career at the Company was to take me irrevocably into the world of aero-engines but I first met Ken Lea soon after he joined Rolls-Royce Motor Cars Ltd as Chief Engineer Power Train and where he was responsible for all engine, driveline and for major parts of chassis engineering together with the military and marine engines.

He led an enthusiastic team of engineers and in a remarkably short time introduced the rationalised fuel-injected-range of engines for the complete range of cars in 1986. When matched to his changes in gearing and other major enhancements to the designs, it made the 1987 Model Year cars and onward some of the most successful produced from Crewe. His work particularly made the Bentley Turbo R an outstanding success which resulted in its becoming a mainstay of the production volume. Even today the Turbo R still enjoys a considerable reputation and following.

In 1987 he was appointed to the Board as Production Director: prior to his joining Rolls-Royce Motor Cars Ltd, he held a similar post in The Leyland

Corporation, Truck and Bus Division.

He left Rolls-Royce Motor Cars Ltd in 1990 but retains his interest and enthusiasm for the cars. He is particularly knowledgeable on Derby Bentleys having owned one for over 25 years, restoring both this and a number of others. A more recent acquisition was a Mk VI which he has also brought back to life and which is much appreciated. Hence his interest in producing this book, the contents of which were given in his lecture at the 50th anniversary celebrations of the first cars from Crewe.

Finally, I would like to refer to the work of Georges Paulin during 1938 and 39 which is described in this publication. I had the opportunity to spend some time with him, at his home in France, just before the outbreak of war and I admired him greatly. That he did not survive the war was a great loss to the Company and was also keenly felt both by my father and myself. His work on the Embiricos Bentley B-27-LE is shown to be key to the success of the Bentley Continental in 1952. This is a fitting and lasting tribute, both to him personally and to his advanced ideas of the time.

Alec Harvey-Bailey
June 1996

PREFACE

This preface is provided for those readers who are not entirely familiar with the history of motor car production at Rolls-Royce Limited to enable them to be clear on the place of the cars described in this book in the history of the Company. I also need to explain why there is frequent reference in the text to particular cars by chassis number as there was, and continues to be, though to a lesser extent, a tradition by all employees to refer to cars by their chassis number, as opposed to their registration. I will take this matter first before providing a brief outline of the history of car production in the Company.

From the very first, all cars were supplied to individuals with coachbuilt bodies. Such was the clientele that cars often changed areas in Britain or travelled abroad. The only safe method of identifying a car, particularly if it was not with its owner, was the unique identifier of the chassis number. Chassis series and number provided that unique identifier in Company circles and for many years the ownership of the chassis was recorded on the chassis card kept at the factory. The advent of more complex chassis numbers or vehicle identification numbers (VINs) today makes this less immediately useable but it remains the only method by which the build specification down to the last nut and bolt can be a identified. Thus, for example, where there was a major derivative, chassis series were amended from A to B to C to D on the Phantom III series cars. To Service and to Engineering departments this initial identifier served to help designate the build of chassis when talking to customers and for parts identification. It was not a foolproof system, as modification control allowed change on a given chassis when it was not a major derivative. Only by reference to the build card could the detail build be found. Thus for those with detail technical knowledge of the product, it was practice to refer to chassis by the complete alpha numeric code. Having worked at the Company for many years, I reverted to type and wrote the book in the chassis series mode. The way it worked is well illustrated in Appendix One where the Mk VI series is described.

Now to an abbreviated history starting with the well-known meeting of Charles Rolls *(CSR)* and Henry Royce *(R)* at the Midland Hotel in Manchester in 1904, which was preceded by the manufacture of the Royce car in Cooke Street, Manchester. Even before the formation of the Company in 1906 there was a series of cars produced in 2-, 3-, 4- and 6-cylinder form but the range was rationalised with the advent of the 40/50 hp Ghost, renowned for its refinement and reliability compared to the standards of the day. The now-famous car registered AX201 was, in fact, the car which bore the name *The Silver Ghost*, which became adopted by the public for all 40/50 hp cars of that model range. AX201 won a Gold Medal in the Scottish

Reliability Trial of 1907, and went on to complete 15,000 miles during that summer, running between London and Glasgow. It was painted silver, and its brightwork was plated in real silver. With the advent of the First World War the Company branched out into aero engine manufacture which was to become all-important in the longer term but, at the end of hostilities in 1918, the production of the Ghost was resumed.

The post-war changes in society were sufficiently profound for the Company, under the astute direction of Claude Johnson (CJ), to design and introduce a small range, known initially as the Goshawk, but launched as the Rolls-Royce Twenty. The Ghost was succeeded in 1925 by the New Phantom which was still a late series Ghost chassis but with a new overhead valve 6-cylinder engine. The Twenty was superseded by the 20/25 in 1929 with the Phantom II replacing the New Phantom at the same time. The Great Depression was gathering momentum and the Company again looked at a more compact owner-driver design, code named Peregrine, which never went to production as a Rolls-Royce, but was nevertheless crucial in development as described later. The 20/25 and Phantom II continued until 1935/6 when they were replaced by the 25/30 and the Phantom III respectively. The former had a larger' engine than its predecessor as increasing body weight demanded a compensating increase in available horsepower and the latter used a novel V-12 7¼ litre engine installed in an advanced chassis with independent front suspension.

In parallel to these developments in the late twenties, Bentley Motors Ltd went into receivership in 1930. The expectation was that the assets would be purchased from the Receiver by D. Napier & Son Ltd who had previously been in car manufacture and who were great competitors of the Company. However, in a surprise but very discrete manoeuvre, Bentley Motors Ltd assets and trademarks were purchased by the Company and Bentley Motors (1931) Ltd was formed as a subsidiary of Rolls-Royce.

To most automotive engineers performance and sporting aspects of the work are always to the fore and the senior staff, including Sir Henry Royce, were no exceptions to this as demonstrated elsewhere in publications in the same series, and shown by the early and lightweight Phantom experimental cars, some production examples of which were sold to technically discerning customers. However, the general public and in particular the old Bentley aficionados were more than surprised at the purchase and there was intense speculation as to whether the Company had purchased the assets and trade name only to prevent its rival re-entering the market. However, a very different Bentley from its predecessors was announced in 1933 and was a 3½ litre engined chassis based on what appeared to be all new designs. The story of the origins of the model and its subsequent derivatives is recounted very clearly in Alec Harvey-Baileys' (AHB's) book, Rolls-Royce – the Derby

Bentleys, also in this series. The car was an instant success and sold exceedingly well, having been finally but enthusiastically developed from a combination of the Peregrine chassis fitted with an experimental 3½ cross-flow head engine code-named J1 and based on the same cylinder centres, bore and stroke of the engine fitted on the 20/25 but which gave considerably more power. The drive train was a variant of the 20/25 gearbox coupled to the Peregrine rear axle.

This model with its later enhancements was in parallel production to the Rolls-Royce cars and aero engines during the thirties with all the products being made at Nightingale Road in Derby.

This now book recounts the history of the subsequent actions taken by the Company from about 1937 with respect to the car business which led to the transfer of car production to their Merlin Shadow Factory at Crewe and to the launch of the new models described here after the Second World War.

K E Lea C Eng, BSc (Hons), FIMechE, MI MarE
September 1996

The first standard bodied Mark VI Bentley, B-6-AK.

THE FIRST CARS FROM CREWE

CHAPTER ONE

The post-war models from Crewe

This book was published to commemorate the launch of production by Rolls-Royce, fifty years earlier in 1946, at their Crewe factory which had been purpose-built in the late thirties to produce piston-type aero-engines, not motor cars.

That car production was destined for Crewe rather than Derby resulted from a decision taken around 1943/44 and the first chassis produced, not surprisingly for those, like myself, who have worked in the industry, was not the first alpha-numerical code B-2-AK, which was the first chassis laid down, as this was not completed until 12 July 1946. One can be sure that it was used within the factory initially for such things as mastering pipes and electrical looming.

The next chassis B-4-AK has a delivery date of 12 February 1946 and hence this was truly the first production Bentley Mark VI chassis to be delivered. In the early months of 1946 production of chassis was very slow, when only three chassis for coachbuilders James Young, H.J.Mulliner and Van den Plas were completed. The first complete car with the standard body from the Pressed Steel Company was B-6-AK, destined to be a showroom car. Chassis completion is not recorded but the complete car was passed to Sales on 21 September 1946. The first two cars B-2-AK and B-4-AK with coachbuilt bodies were also passed to Sales on the same date, presumably for the Motor Show at Earls Court in 1946. It was of interest to learn that B-4-AK and B-2-AK still survive and are in the process of being restored.

The first Rolls-Royce Silver Wraith chassis, number WTA-1, was completed on 20 May 1946 and when bodied was also passed to Sales on 21 September 1946. The first of that rare model, the Rolls-Royce Phantom IV, chassis number 4-AF-2, was not produced until 20 July 1949, destined for use by HRH Princess Elizabeth and HRH Prince Philip.

The Rolls-Royce Silver Dawn was also a much later product, the first being chassis number LSBA-2, a left-hand-drive car, completed and passed to Sales on the 26th. April 1949.

Rolls-Royce Silver Wraith similar to WTA-1.

Rolls-Royce Phantom IV 4-AF-8, which was supplied to the Emir of Kuwait.

Rolls-Royce Silver Dawn, thought to be LSBA-2, heads a line of Bentley VIs awaiting despatch at Crewe.

Sir Henry Royce.

CHAPTER TWO

People and policies

Hostilities in Europe finished in May 1945 and hence the production of these new models in such a short time appeared nothing short of miraculous, especially as, in motor car terms, the Company was seen as somewhat conservative. Even those clients who were used to purchasing the Company's products could see little resemblance to the pre-war Bentley 4¼ litre, or even the more modern in design concept Rolls-Royce Wraith which featured independent suspension but whose design features had something in common with the Phantom III. These new models were exciting not just because of their new chassis concepts but because, for the first time in the Company's history, the range included a complete car. This announcement was to have a profound and deleterious effect on the traditional coachbuilding industry.

To find out how Rolls-Royce moved so quickly, one must research the Company's activities prior to the onset of hostilities in September 1939, which reveals that, in truth, the story is actually much older even than this.

E.W.Hives *(Hs)*, later to become Lord Hives, strong and well focused.

It could be said that with the death of Sir Henry Royce *(R)* in 1933, the overall guiding hand, at least in engineering terms, of this most eminent but practical of engineers was lost and this had a profound effect on the Company but it was an effect that took some time to manifest itself. It was clear that no one person could replace him and by the mid-thirties there were ominous signs with the Company suffering high manufacturing costs, a disparate model range with teams only working loosely together and with both engineering and manufacturing resources spread too thinly. Product reliability, whilst not perhaps overtly recognised due to the Company's approach to customers, was not satisfactory, with the Phantom III being launched too early in its development and the 4¼ litre Bentley in 1936-37 being plagued with bearing problems especially when used on long hard running on the Continent.

When E.W. Hives *(Hs)* was appointed as General Manager in 1936, he faced the task of eliminating these problems and of restoring the Company's trading position. He embarked on a rapid programme of problem resolution, for such problems as exampled above, as well as a full review of the organisation of the Company to meet its future needs. *Hs* was determined that the cost base of the Company on both the chassis and aero-engine sides of the business must be drastically reduced and that engineering resources must be more radically focused. After much heart-searching he determined to divide Engineering into two divisions, a radical concept because it moved against the philosophy that all engineering staffs were integrated, moving from project to project as directed. This particularly applied to the senior personnel involved. The Aero Engine Division was to be led for Engineering by A.G.Elliott *(E)* who had previously been in overall charge of Engineering as Chief Engineer. His counterpart was something of a surprise to his contemporaries, but nevertheless because of this person's close work with *R* and *Hs* over many years, the latter had no doubt who he wanted to appoint as Chief Engineer of the newly-formed Chassis Division. He appointed R.W.Harvey-Bailey *(By)* to this post. Here was a man who had a proven record in engineering terms but also supplemented this with a strong affinity for materials and for matters of production.

R.W. Harvey-Bailey *(By)*, proven extremely capable but not an extrovert.

W.A.Robotham *(Rm)*, well-liked by his staff, very capable but sometimes difficult.

CHAPTER THREE

The new philosophy

The problems faced by *By* were large, but he was ably supported by W.A.Robotham *(Rm)*. There soon emerged a proposal to meet the product requirements and the reduction in manufacturing costs. This was to adopt a philosophy of common units being applied across a series of different chassis for each market/model, these also designed to utilise common components such as pressings, suspensions, steering, brakes, instruments and so on. In his scheme, there was to be a new series of engines code-named the 'B-range'. Within the 'Rationalised Range'of cars, for that was its code name, the new engines would be available in 4-, 6- and 8-cylinder in-line form with an added flexibility derived from different cylinder bore sizes.

A further facet of the proposal was derived from the Company's deep dissatisfaction with the design standards of the coachbuilders, in terms of noise, rattles and particularly weight. These long-established firms fitted bodies without exception to all the Company's products and, of course, standards varied widely and were of the customer's choice. However, any quality problems naturally reflected on the Company rather than the bodybuilder. It was proposed to adopt a range of standard bodies in conjunction with Park Ward Ltd who were taken over by the Company in 1938. It was an ambitious plan with many attendant risks, but after intensive review and debate, *Hs* accepted the strategy as the competitive pressures were all too real from such companies as Alvis, Lagonda, Daimler, Delahaye etc. It was from this new strategy, born of a thorough understanding of the needs of the Company, by the principals in office in 1937, that the evolution of the first cars manufactured at Crewe can be traced and it was these decisions that allowed the introduction of entirely new models so soon after the war in Europe.

In 1937 two priorities determined the first models to be designed and built experimentally. The first was the replacement of the Bentley 4¼ litre which, although it had sold well and was a well-balanced product, was now becoming dated in its design, lacking such improvements as independent front suspension and a torsionally rigid frame with their contribution to enhanced ride and handling. The second was for the replacement of the Phantom III which was an extremely expensive chassis to produce and which had cost the Company dear in other ways.

Thus business needs dictated the early priorities, in design and development terms, of the new Rationalised Range. However, it is my experience that the philosophy of rationalisation is a periodic phenomenon natural to engineers when beset by too much product complexity,

Both Bentley 4¼ and the earlier 3½ were successful and well-balanced competent cars.

The Phantom III, a marvellous concept, launched too early and expensive to produce.

The commonised 4¼ litre engine for 1937 to about 1940 shown here in Rolls-Royce Wraith specification.

26

accompanied by the realisation that resources are finite. Its precursor is often design ingenuity fuelled by a wealth of experience and the natural desires of the Sales Department to have product differentiation.

Neither can it be achieved instantaneously but some crisis in design philosophy can be its catalyst. It seems that this was so when, in 1937, *Hs* reviewed the progress on the 25/30 model replacement. As early as 1935, decisions were made to replace the small-horsepower range and work had begun as a matter of urgency. Although chassis design was completed, no decision was made as to the engine configuration as late as mid 1937 and even though the first experimental car was running, it used the existing 25/30 engine. Schemes were in hand for a small sixty-degree V-12 cylinder layout, followed by a ninety degree V-8 making a straight or in-line 8 a low priority. It was then found that any V-8 scheme of merit would not fit behind the 'Ionic' radiator. It appears to be this indecision by *E* that was the catalyst for the acceptance of a rationalised engine concept, as time was now pressing.

Although the 4¼ litre Bentley engine had suffered bearing problems, detailed development had overcome these and much more was also known about the engine speed limiting third-order torsional vibration. This could be raised by stiffening the crankshaft webs, itself made possible by new R-R main bearing materials that allowed the width of the bearing to be reduced. An increase in diameter of the main bearings also contributed to crankshaft stiffness in torsion. Power output was significantly superior to its 25/30 counterpart, partially due to the superior limit of 'detonation' characteristic of the 'bathtub' combustion chamber. A decision was taken between *Hs* and *By* to fit all Rolls-Royce and Bentley models, with the exception of the Phantom III, with a rationalised 6-cylinder overhead-valve engine on the same cylinder centres and the same bore and stroke as the 4¼ litre Bentley engine and incorporating many of its features. Without doubt, this decision was influenced by the lead-times required and the ability to use existing tooling and machinery.

The cylinder head design would retain the cross-flow feature but, in order to accommodate both twin- and single-carburettor systems, the six-inlet port design was deliberately sacrificed for a siamesed porting system giving four inlets. The three siamesed exhaust ports were retained. It also had a three-gear camshaft and distributor drive as opposed to five with the distributor necessarily mounted on the camshaft side. The major revisions to the crankshaft to increase the engine working speed range were also featured with the stiffer webs and bigger diameter, but narrower main bearings. The position of the water pump was also moved to the rear to improve waterflow at the rear of the engine.

Thus the first product of the newly formed Chassis Division was the 25/30 Wraith with an all-welded cruciform frame, independent front suspension

Bentley 4¼ litre OHC design run both on the bed and in a car. It owed much promise but was not favoured, not least for the camshaft drive arrangement.

and the first variant of the commonised engine. It was released for manufacture in mid 1937 ready for the announcement at the Motor Show. Significantly, for the later models in the rationalised design, this common engine was demonstrably capable of varying power output by varying valve size, camshaft lift and period, twin or single carburettors and higher compression ratios. It was clear that this engine must power the range apart from Phantom III until the new B-range engine was developed: it was not scheduled for production until at least 1940/41.

With the final development of the Wraith, the Chassis Division were now free to take up the new direction to design a new range of motor cars and no development of the Wraith concept for a Bentley replacement was made. The next Bentley, initially named Bentley III, but later changed to Bentley V, was the first product of the new direction and in chassis terms differed significantly from the Wraith. More of Bentley V later, but first some more on the new B-range engine developments.

It is said that little is new in conceptual terms in engineering and here to my mind is such an example. The desire for more power, necessitating larger valves, was risking cylinder head integrity which was limited by a foundry's ability to maintain sound metal in the valve bridge area between the valve seats. It is a given that either cylinder centres had to increase, thus reducing crankshaft stiffness in torsion so that the critical speed was again reduced and, not least, incurring expensive tooling and machinery changes, or some new breathing and combustion configuration had to be found. The chosen configuration, after a detailed review including the previous work on a single-overhead-camshaft design of the 4¼ which had shown much promise, was to adopt an overhead inlet valve and side exhaust valve which thus maintained the cylinder centres but eliminated the critical design limitation on the cylinder head. In the ensuing years there has been considerable speculation that this concept was adopted from the last model of the old Bentley Motors Company, namely, the ill-fated 4-litre employing a Ricardo design of the same type. However, to illustrate my point, *R* had himself employed this configuration in 1903! In truth, I can find no evidence that the premise is true and its adoption seems to stem more from the theme of "necessity is the mother of invention". Alec Harvey-Bailey *(AHB)* is clear that Colonel Barrington *(Bn)*, who had transferred from the old company, Bentley Motors Ltd, had insufficient influence to direct policy and even W.O. Bentley himself was not enthusiastic about the Ricardo engine.

The new B-range engine had a heavier cast-iron integral crankcase which is anathema from the weight standpoint but it had been previously tried in earlier experimental engines, where notable improvements in refinement were seen. This weight increase was partially offset by the employment of an aluminium cylinder head. A single-cylinder engine was running in 1937 and the design of the engine was completed quickly during this same year, utilising the stiffer crankshaft concepts of the commonised engine but having a two-gear camshaft drive. The adoption of the newly available copper-lead bearings for both mains and big-ends was also featured. It retained the inlet port configuration of the commonised engine. A 3¼-inches-bore engine was also incorporated at this time alongside the 3½ inch of the 4¼ litre, with the first B60 engine being installed in a Wraith in early 1938. This was probably only for initial assessment rather than with any production intentions, as the Wraith design was to be superseded by the new range.

In parallel, the Bentley chassis was designed, being the first model of the new concept, but still differing from the final specification from the full rationalised range with such notable exceptions as the engine and having all

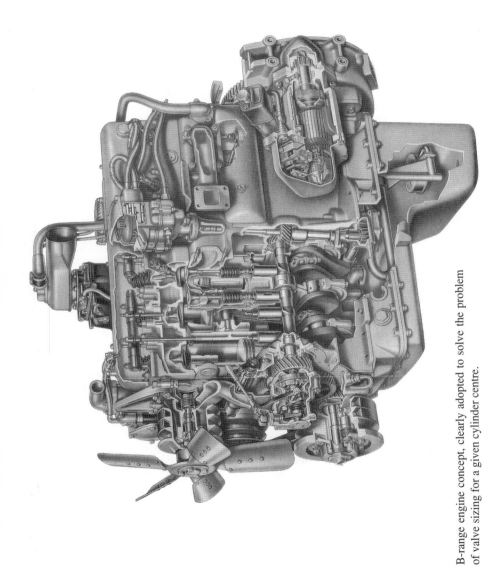

B-range engine concept, clearly adopted to solve the problem of valve sizing for a given cylinder centre.

Bentley V chassis layout. The first of a fundamental change in design approach.

mechanically operated brakes as opposed to the hydraulic actuation of the front brakes envisaged. It did incorporate a new overdrive gearbox featuring synchromesh on second gear and a rationalised axle design which was designed to incorporate strengthened half-shafts and wheel-hub drives as well an improved semi-floating axle shaft for use with steel disc wheels and a hypoid differential design. The chassis was again of cruciform construction but was riveted as opposed to all-welded as seen on the Wraith. Incidentally, such were the difficulties, in manufacturing terms, of the all-welded design that it was not introduced again until on the R-type in the mid 50s. The independent suspension moved from horizontally mounted coil springs, as seen on Phantom III and the Wraith, to vertically mounted coils and with the suspension directly mounted on the frame as opposed to a separate and expensive unit.

The first car, shown outside the home of *Rm*, was a remarkably handsome car but still employing running-boards and swept wings with the associated narrower passenger compartment. The Experimental Department was quick to praise the car as a chassis of great potential and further cars were quickly built, with continental testing well underway in 1938 where 8-B-V is shown in the picture. Other cars of differing body styles were added to the experimental fleet and Bentley V, probably the most thoroughly developed and tested car the company had seen, was ready for sale and released to production well in time for announcement at the usual venue of the Motor Show in 1939. Several cars featured the 'standard' Rolls-Royce steel body built by Park Ward as shown fitted to 9-B-V in production form. Also illustrated is an early version of the drophead as fitted to chassis 10-B-V. Albeit, the production of chassis was well under way by mid 1939 and output was increasing.

The second priority was to replace the Phantom III and the first experimental car was also on the road later in 1938 and was affectionately known as 'Big Bertha'. The Phantom III replacement was intended for production in 1940 having an 11ft 1in wheelbase, some 3 inches shorter than the Wraith, only slightly heavier but giving Phantom III-like performance from the first installation of the 5.3 litre 8-cylinder in-line B80 engine. This was an early indication that the benefits of the new programme were real, as exampled by *Rm*'s comment that this was the best car that the Company had ever built, its balance of characteristics making it a delight on the road. The enthusiasm for the 8-cylinder was further enhanced when a Bentley prototype, code-named 'Comet', utilising the shortest chassis of the range, like the Bentley V, was built as part of the rationalised concept of matching different engines to the three wheelbase lengths of 10ft 4in, 10ft 10in and 11ft 1in to produce a wider range of cars of both marques. 11-B-V was another instant demonstration of the inherent capability of the concept,

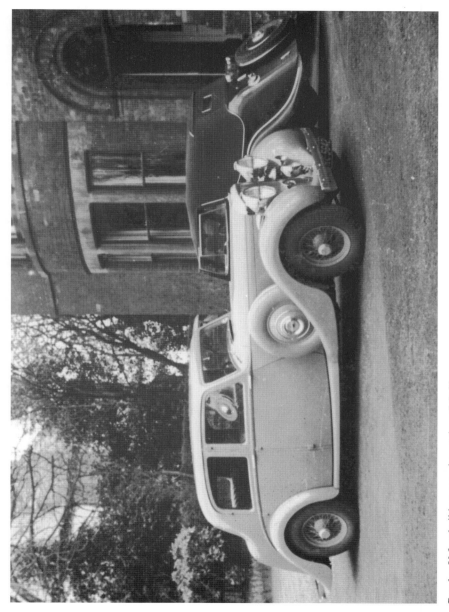

Bentley V first build as experimental car 7-B-V.

coupled with short lead-times and reduced development and road testing costs. 11-B-V was known as the 'Scalded Cat' because of its electrifying acceleration and both these cars captivated all who drove them. The Phantom III replacement lapped Brooklands at 91 mph with a 7-seater limousine body, with very good performance noted in the 80 to 90 mph range. The Scalded Cat, initially fitted with a single Stromberg twin-choke carburettor, was further uprated by fitting three 1½in-bore SU carburettors. Its power-to-weight ratio coupled with an overall gearing ratio of 3.115:1 gave an easy 100 mph at 3820 rpm.

Bentley V 8-B-V on test on the Continent in 1938.

The standard production body on chassis 9-B-V.

10-B-V, an experimental drophead used for a time during the war by Air Marshal "Bomber" Harris.

Phantom III's scheduled successor, known as 'Big Bertha', delighted *Rm*.

The electrifying 'Scalded Cat', Bentley 11-B-V.

Bentley 4¼ litre B-27-LE, the Embiricos car – body designed by Paulin, built by Partout.

CHAPTER FOUR

The performance factor

Before the story of the initial models of the Rationalised Range can be concluded, there is one other facet that requires illustration as this was instrumental in policy terms much later in the 1950s. The advent of the autobahns in Germany in the 1930s forever changed peoples' perception of what was required to travel from A to B. As well as sustained reliability, a growing number of clients wanted higher cruising speeds and a Bentley well capable of over 100 mph.

In 1938 the Company was involved with a 4¼ litre Bentley chassis number B-27-LE, known as the Embiricos Bentley, fitted with a streamlined body designed by a Frenchman, Georges Paulin, and built by a small company, again French, named Pourtout. The engine was uprated, using features from the experience with the Eddie Hall car B-35-AE which had been raced. The chassis had a higher-ratio back axle, an M-series overdrive gearbox and the engine had a modest increase in compression ratio and larger carburettors. Its performance, compared to standard cars with traditional bodies, was so significant that it was brought to Derby for evaluation after testing on the Continent.

Both *By* and *Rm* were enthusiastic and *By* and others had an immediate rapport with Paulin. *By* and *Rm* seized the chance to improve the image of Bentley in the face of competition from the V-12 Lagonda which had W.O. Bentley's involvement. The car was tested on the track both at Brooklands and at Montlhery and was timed at 114.6 miles in the hour with 10 miles at 115 mph when driven by George Eyston.

By proposed that here was an opportunity to fulfil the requirements of their customers which was a view strongly supported by Walter Sleator *(Sr)* from Franco-Britannique Automobiles, Paris. The fact that the traditional headlights and radiator were proven to absorb too much power was resisted by the Board who thought the style too *avant garde*. Obviously power from the 6-cylinder engine was limited but it was also tuned for high torque over a wide speed range rather than top-end power but *By* proposed that a more economical use of the power available was to adopt lightweight streamlined bodies in order to achieve the customer demands. Fortunately he won the day, but rather than develop the M-series 4¼ litre car, as its production life was limited, the policy was to introduce a high-performance version of Bentley V. The policy, having been accepted, was to launch this new car alongside the standard Bentley V at the 1939 Motor Show. The body was to be designed by Paulin under the direction of H.I.F. Evernden *(Ev)* who worked for *By* and who was also responsible for the styling of the standard

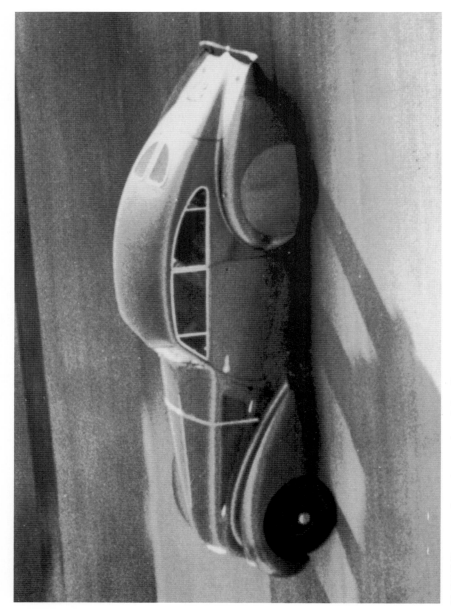

B-27-LE at speed on the track at Monthery.

range of bodies being introduced at Park-Ward. The bodies were to be built, at least initially, by Van Vooren who were amongst the best in terms of weight control, but under the supervision of Paulin.

By the late spring of 1939, the prototype 14-B-V was complete. The low-drag body of pillarless construction was both light but taut and at the same time roomy with good egress and ingress. The car, called Corniche, weighed in at 34 hundredweights, but benefiting from a modest uprating of the OHV 4¼ litre rationalised engine, a low-loss dual exhaust system, overdrive gearbox and a higher ratio axle, it soon dispelled any lingering doubts by lapping Brooklands at 109 mph with 111 mph demonstrated on a flying mile. The car is also shown on test in France in the summer of 1939 but it was then involved in a serious crash and repairs were commenced but never completed. Nevertheless, because sufficient confidence had been gained with a promised 115 mph capability provided by *Rm*, production specifications were released in June and production commenced with at least six chassis issued for build and in progress by September 1939.

The importance of aerodynamic drag was clearly recognised and, to *By* and his team, streamlining was now a fact of life, affecting ideas of standard body design. An early example of this evolution was an 8-cylinder rationalised prototype 4-B-50 code-named 'Cresta' with integral headlights. A combination of this and the standard body styled by *Ev* and as mounted on 9-B-V for Bentley V gives clear direction to the later styling of the Mark VI shown in the photograph as a wooden mock up or styling buck, thought to be circa 1944/5.

Bentley V Corniche with Van Vooren body, chassis 14-B-V.

44

14-B-V on test in the summer of 1939 in France.

Bentley Cresta – a rationalised car with revised headlight styling shown just after the outbreak of war.

Bentley Mk VI styling mock-up in wood at Clan Foundry, Belper circa 1944.

The intended Phantom III successor – known as 'Big Bertha'.

CHAPTER FIVE

The results of the new philosophy in September 1939

To finally return to the pre-war period, one can summarise the progress made by *By* and his staff by analysing the overall achievement which was that by September 1939 Bentley V and its performance version the Corniche were in production thoroughly developed and tested and ready for announcement at the 1939 Motor Show. In addition there were several examples of the true Rationalised Range built and on test including the Phantom III replacement and what is generally thought to be the Wraith replacement built as a Bentley chassis number 3-B-50, which was a 10ft 10in-wheelbase car but fitted with a twin carburetted version of the B60 engine. Other exciting models were contemplated for the 1940 Motor Show, such as an 8-cylinder Corniche as well as the replacements for the Wraith and Phantom III.

When *Hs* separated chassis work from that of aero-engines in 1937, he took a calculated decision, not without risk, in choosing the people tasked to revitalise the car business and his contemporary board reports reflect this. However, the practical evidence was that, within two years, he had two new engines, the first a rationalised derivative of the 4¼ Bentley, the second all new, new units and chassis evidenced by eleven experimental cars built covering six models including two in production by August 1939. The costs were demonstrably lower and the prospects of adequate margins were in sight. The fortunes of the Chassis Division looked set fair when viewed from a Company standpoint and his confidence in *By* and his staff, including *Rm* and *Ev*, was well justified.

The advent of hostilities in early September 1939 had two immediate effects, the first being that car production rapidly ceased and secondly that the 1939 Motor Show was cancelled. Hence Bentley V and Corniche were never officially announced, which resulted in the survival of only a few Bentley Vs. It is a sad fact that, rightly or wrongly with hindsight, all production Corniches and 14-B-V chassis were scrapped during the war as were many incomplete Bentley Vs. There were many rumours about the fate of the Corniche, including the story that the whole car was destroyed by enemy action. The record shows that the body was removed by the coachbuilder upon which repairs were commenced and the chassis was shipped separately to Derby for repairs in parallel, as the car was wanted urgently for final work and for exhibition. It was the repaired body complete with keys in the switch-box that was destroyed by enemy action on the docks in France.

However, *Hs* held the Chassis Division team together until about 1940,

3-B-50 thought to be the Wraith replacement in chassis terms.

but it was eventually redirected onto fighting-vehicle work. There was one immediate exception to this, it being when *Hs* expressly instructed *By* to transfer back to Merlin engine work and *Rm* was appointed Chief Engineer of the Chassis Division. All engineering functions were transferred to Clan Foundry soon after the outbreak of war. *By* was never to return to cars as he retired in 1946 at the age of 68, having served as always, with great distinction and dedication on his last assignment. It is a tribute to him that he was recognised by everyone, both internally and externally, for example from Ford and Packard who built the Merlin during the war and many sent personal tributes acclaiming his legendary skills in pragmatic achievement. To him, above all others, must go the credit for the inception and early development of the Rationalised Range.

Rm too departed, although somewhat later, when he was seconded to the Ministry of Supply, but he remained in the employ of the Company, returning in the latter part of 1943. He again led Chassis Division engineering until its transfer to Crewe in the late forties, but he eventually led the design and development of the R-R C-range of oil engines – a diesel to the rest of us but not to him! It was he who was responsible for the design of the first post-war models and for the development in thinking about the wider concepts of the Rationalised Range which were eventually to come to naught with respect to the smaller cars envisaged.

Harry Grylls *(Gry)* – regarded as somewhat aloof and by some as a cynic.

CHAPTER SIX

Policies and developments for post-war cars

The Chassis Division engineering work recommenced in strategic terms in late 1943, housed at Clan Foundry, and continued under the direction of *Rm* who reported directly to *Hs* for all his tenure as Chief Engineer. When Engineering transferred to Crewe during 1948/9 it was led by Harry Grylls *(Gry)*.

One of the first tasks was to review and re-instate the Rationalised Range and various modifications to the model range were made. In 1939 the name Clipper was the code name for Bentley V and the name Cresta was applied to a model built as 4-B-50. This model was dropped and the name Cresta was applied to a variant of the original Clipper in the 1944 range and the car 4-B-50 was dismantled. The new Cresta had a wheelbase of 10ft 6in, and still took the 6- and 8-cylinder engines. This model was further revised in 1945 when the front end dimension, which is from centreline of the front wheels to the dashboard, was reduced by 6 inches, making the wheelbase 10ft 0in but still specifying the 6-and 8- cylinder engines. The 6-cylinder version was to become the Mk VI and hence it is clear that the Mk VI is truly a product of the Rationalised Range and, because of its antecedents with Bentley V and features of the 4-B-50 chassis cars, this explains why the chassis could be launched so quickly after the war. A note to explain the 6-inch reduction which is that it was introduced to increase further the torsional and bending stiffness in the frame as experience with the experimental drophead 10-B-V had shown that severe scuttle shake was present when the contribution that the saloon bodies made to stiffness was reduced. The view was that this was at the expense of ride and handling, as those who drove both said the Bentley V was somewhat superior in this respect.

Similar adjustment of the parallel launch design of the Rolls-Royce Silver Wraith resulted in a production chassis with a wheelbase of 10ft 7in but it only specified the 6-cylinder engine as opposed to Cresta which specified both 6 and 8. However, whilst it is clear that the Company still wished to pursue the 8-cylinder engine for cars, the social upheavals caused by the election of the Socialist Government stayed their hand in launching such a model in the early post-war years. Similarly for the same 'political' reasons the Bentley marque became both central and crucial to the survival of the Chassis Division and hence it became the production volume mainstay right throughout the life of the Rationalised Range production models for both home and traditional British export markets.

Various major projects were commenced in parallel and encompassed the three elements of the chassis and engine release to production, the build-up of the necessary production facilities and a fundamental decision to produce a complete motor car utilising a standard body shell: the body to be painted, trimmed and the whole car completed at the factory concerned. This meant the adoption of new skills with which the Company had only a loose association in production terms, although they had become increasingly involved in body engineering in the late thirties to provide taut but lighter-weight structures. This work had been done in conjunction with Park Ward. Coachbuilt bodies would still be acceptable and the Rolls-Royce Silver Wraith model would not take the standard body type.

The first decision concerned the chassis specification and two elements of the Rationalised Range not seen on Bentley V, viz. the B-range engine and hydraulically actuated front brakes, were adopted as a result of the mileage and experience gained during the war. However, whilst the engine range was being tooled in full for the various cylinder numbers of 4, 6 and 8, initial production on all models was limited to the 4¼ litre 6-cylinder engine. This engine was regarded as proven although, with the benefit of hindsight, it is clear that the low octane rating of emergency fuels and no chance to develop performance had masked a problem that was to prove difficult to eradicate or even understand until well into the 50s. This is dealt with, together with other engine matters, in Chapter Seven. The basic units were from the pre-war specifications but for reasons that are not entirely clear the overdrive concept of overall gearing so successfully employed on the M-series Bentley 4¼ and on the later Phantom IIIs was replaced by a direct-drive top gearbox and a change in axle ratio to 11:41. One can only surmise that, for the overall weight, the needs of acceleration were seen as more important than cruising capability in the immediate post-war environment.

It is perhaps significant that the first prototype, 1-B-VI, did not perform well initially and certainly in back-to-back comparisons with the well-worn 3-B-50 and a Bentley V showed its first performance assessment to be inferior in both acceleration and top speed. Perhaps it was a precautionary measure but sufficient to say that by the time the cars were ready for sale, performance was acceptable.

The second decision was that production of cars would be centred at the Crewe factory, which had been specifically built to manufacture the variants of the V-12 Merlin and the later Griffon reciprocating piston aero-engines. The need for volume production of these engines was passing rapidly with the last Griffon 89 being produced there on the 1st. December 1945. A new use for Crewe must be found either as gas turbine component producer or to produce another product. History shows that the Crewe factory, already in limited production of such components, was chosen to produce completely the car range except where coachbuilt bodies were ordered, and the changeover commenced in 1945. It was *Hs* who decided that aero-engine

The original Bentley Cresta, chassis number 4-B-50.

The first prototype Bentley Mk VI fitted with a coachbuilt body by Mulliner – chassis 1-B-VI.

A contemporary aerial view of the Crewe factory.

products would be dominant after the war and, as Derby was the largest site, it should be the centre of this work. Rolls-Royce owned the Crewe site but only managed the Glasgow shadow factory and hence it was the obvious choice. One rather amusing anecdote was that *Hs*'s view of the Derby Works was still somewhat jaundiced as he felt that cars should go to Crewe as "there were still too many employees with expensive habits."

The third decision already referred to earlier was to manufacture a standard body made from steel pressings and jig assembled. Although such techniques were in lower volume production at Park Ward from about 1936 onwards, the decision was made to leave Park Ward to traditional coachbuilt bodies and to transfer the project to the Pressed Steel Company at Cowley. This decision had far-reaching effects on the long-term future of the traditional body builders previously used, but the Company felt that for the volumes and quality required, such skills as were required, were best bought from a company used to larger capacity steel body production. By December 1945 panel definition was complete and tooling under way, evidenced by a concise engineering report provided by the Pressed Steel Company. This culminated in the second prototype Mk VI, chassis number 2-B-VI, being fitted with the first all-steel standard body.

Although the Mk VI chassis was available for coachbuilt bodies, such bodies were twice the cost of the standard body. With the Socialist Government hostile to luxury cars and the name of Rolls-Royce in particular, this was made worse by the imposition of a $66^2/_3\%$ purchase tax on cars over £1000. *Hs* did not commit to large production numbers but this did allow time to absorb the steep learning experience of manufacturing a complete car, made that much more difficult by the retirement of many of the engineers with chassis and body experience at the end of the war.

Body panel divisions for the standard steel body for pressed tool manufacture.

The first standard steel body mounted on the second prototype 2-B-VI.

The last chassis as a 4¼ litre, B-401-LH still in regular use, having covered some 130,000 miles by June 1996.

CHAPTER SEVEN

The evolution of the post-war range

The launch of the Bentley Mk VI and the Rolls-Royce Silver Wraith was successful and, in parallel with the increase in volume of the models, a programme of continuous improvement commenced, although the standard 4¼ litre Mk VI Bentley remained in production until June 1951 when the last car, B-401-LH, currently in the author's possession, was completed.

The sale of cars outside the United Kingdom also climbed steadily and, to aid this, a left-hand-drive version was also introduced. In service, export use identified cooling problems and the modifications, listed in total in Appendix One, featured a larger-area radiator and changes to the radiator fixed vanes to increase airflow. Although there were other chassis changes to the suspension, many of the early modifications centred on the body, with changes to seals, window mechanisms and channels and the heater system. There were also a series of modifications to the engine, with changes to piston and rings, cylinder head gaskets and some evidence that there was too wide a spread of power on production engines which was rectified by the introduction of graded-compression-height pistons.

Turning now to more engine matters, when first developed and released for manufacture, the B60 was fitted with a by-pass oil filter common to that fitted pre-war to the 4¼ litre Bentley overdrive-series cars. This filter kept the oil looking remarkably clean, but the copper lead bearings proved much less tolerant of dirt than their softer pre-war counterparts and a number of big-end bearing failures were seen in service. Furthermore, although reliable in everyday use, the chrome-plate flash to the top of the parent cylinder bore only lasted about 40,000 miles in some cases, as opposed to 80-90,000 miles seen on experimental engines. This was the difference between meticulous in-house servicing and, in some cases, a rather more lackadaisical approach on the part of owners, coupled with different duty cycles. The B-range engine had by this time also become a standard military engine, which had a full-flow filter specified. This had proved much more effective, and pointed the way for change. To combat the cylinder bore wear problem a short liner insert in a material called 'chromard' was introduced on chassis number B-144-DA.

Work on improving B60 engine performance was also undertaken, but the simple method of increasing power by raising compression ratio even modestly produced no more power, a little more low speed torque and much combustion roughness. Clearly its cause was not understood and the demands for more power and torque were met by increasing the bore to 3 ⅝ths-inches diameter. This was difficult to achieve as it meant the siamesing of the cylinder barrels along the longitudinal centreline of the engine and needed considerable piston development, with new machining techniques being required by the piston supplier. The 7% increase in engine capacity fortuitously allowed a more advantageous combustion chamber shape, although the reason was not appreciated until much later, but power increased more than to be expected to 153 hp as opposed to 145. This was achieved with the same carburettor needle specification as the 4¼ litre engine and, hence, it was clear, with hindsight, that the combustion chamber shape was the significant factor as opposed to gas flow restrictions in the porting. It was not until the later engines in the S-series cars that the restriction was identified as choking at the throat around the exhaust valve.

Thus was born the 4½ litre specification which continued with the chromard material insert to the top of the bore but now included the adoption of full-flow filtration. This engine, in customers' hands, proved significantly more durable and it was introduced on M-series chassis, together with a twin-pipe exhaust system. The chromard liner insert itself was eventually superseded by fitting a full-length liner both on the 4.9 litre engine and for service. However, in 1951 a Service Bulletin was issued for older engines to take full-flow filtration and the liner collar. Service kits were made available and many older engines were converted at overhaul.

The significance of low-loss exhaust systems was known in the late thirties, but for some reason this knowledge, perhaps through the perception of an overriding need for Rolls-Royce standards of refinement even on the Bentley as it was the mainstay of production, was not transferred onto the 4¼ Mk VI and it was found that the single-pipe system on production absorbed some 28 hp from that given with an open exhaust! This was much greater than the dual systems seen on Corniche and 3-B-50, for example, and work on the twin system reduced this power absorption to some 9 hp, but at a cost of being expensive and difficult to install. The Mk VI M- through P-series cars introduced in 1951, and later known colloquially as the 'big bore/small boot Bentley', benefited from these changes and were the first production cars from the Company truly capable of over 100 mph.

Turning for a moment to the developments of the Rolls-Royce models, market demand from abroad led to the later introduction of the previously planned standard steel bodied version but which had been delayed by the resistance to the Rolls-Royce name being widely used on cars by Government officials and where the development of the aircraft engine business was thus at risk. The first experimental car, 1-SD-I, featuring the intended square-cornered bonnet and scuttle code-named in 1945 'Ascot I', together with a 3½ litre version of the B60 engine was on the road in July 1947. A second car, 2-SD-II, fitted with the Ascot II body shell common to the Mk VI was built by July 1948. Although this car covered little mileage as

The prototype 1-SD-I with its originally envisaged differing body shell to Ascot I standard.

The second experimental car 2-SD -II to production specification using the Ascot II body common to Mk VI.

an experimental car, it proved the basis of the production specification of the Silver Dawn which featured a single Stromberg carburetted 4¼ litre B60, common to Silver Wraith. Many early Silver Dawns were left-hand drive, destined for the United States where they proved relatively popular. The Silver Wraith and the Silver Dawn received similar modifications to Bentley Mk VI where appropriate and both vehicles adopted the 4½ litre engine, but again with the single carburettor and the single exhaust system to maintain traditional 'Rolls-Royce' refinement.

The mighty 8-cylinder engine, whose inherent design characteristics made it smooth and not subject to the torsional limitations of the 6-cylinder, was now in volume production on the military and commercial markets, but saw no use in car production apart from the introduction of the Phantom IV, a car of 12ft 1in wheelbase where the 8-cylinder B80 engine was fitted again with the single Stromberg carburettor. Because of the political aspects, these cars were rare indeed as only 12 were made for Heads of State. The two made for the Royal Household are pictured here together with other Household Phantoms of later date.

However, in some of the senior remaining Engineering Department staff, including *Rm* and *Ev*, the 8-cylinder remained a fervent wish, even to the extent that a second Scalded Cat, 2-SC-1 was built, adopting the Scalded Cat image as its experimental code. This car was built on production at Crewe, using a standard body but with extended bonnet and wings. When fitted with an aluminium crankcase version of the B80, the kerbside weight was 37¾ hundredweights. However, it was then fitted with a cast iron crankcase 3⅝-inches-bore engine giving, with SU carburettors, some 200 hp. But such was the continuing austerity of the country in its post-war social environment, and in the face of resistance from the Car Division's Managing Director, F. Llewellyn-Smith *(LS)*, and even from *Gry*, no plans for production were successful.

By 1949 the Mk VI was also subject to criticism on two further aspects in addition to the low power criticism, the first being for heating and ventilation and the second for very limited luggage space brought on by gradual easing of social attitudes and with less restriction on travel. In a report of February 1951, *Ev* reflects on this change in requirement, and I quote one statement from the report which reads "Today a family wishes no longer to share a cabin trunk, each member desires an individual piece of luggage". The days of the old fold-down boot lid designed for the carriage of the said trunk were clearly numbered especially as competitive products such as Jaguar Mk VII and American cars were offering larger enclosed compartments. As ever time was short, so tooling changes were limited though early foresight in the design of the body in 1944 allowed such changes to be made relatively simply.

Ev comments further when outlining his specification, and again I quote directly from his report, "Womenfolk always have personal luggage such as hat boxes, dressing cases and shoe cases, which they insist on taking with them on the journey." It really does seem for us men that some things in life are a constant if personal experience is anything to go by! Experiments were conducted on a 'standardised' set of luggage and here the Mk VI was said to have only effectively 6 cubic feet capacity. The revisions, by using a top hinged boot lid, modifying the spare wheel stowage, altering the petrol tank and extending the body and the chassis by 6 inches behind the axle, resulted in a most pleasing and handsome car which gave the Mk VI an extended model life whilst work, already running late, on the next car range could proceed. Luggage capacity was now some 10.5 cubic feet and this resulted in new panelling from the rear door pillar (C-post) and new rear wings. Spats to the rear wheels were deleted.

These changes to the rear overhang forced a change to the rear springs which were extended and inclined to provide extra roll-understeer. The general specification included automatic choke to the carburettors, two speed windscreen wipers and a hot and cold demister system, although this appeared on the last P-series chassis of the Mk VI. A full revision to the heating and ventilation system was impossible to engineer economically in this configuration of body and this had to wait for the S-series cars. In addition the start of a fundamental change for the longer term was an option to fit a 4-speed automatic gearbox. This version was launched in 1952 as the R-type Bentley, not as the Mk VII as it was code-named and, in production terms, ran until early 1955. It was a very successful and popular car in all markets, by now mature and durable, but by 1955 considered somewhat dated both in style and in its specification.

Two Rolls-Royce Phantom IVs built for use by the Royal Household seen with later versions of Phantoms.

The second 'Scalded Cat' – the engineer's dream, but a victim of politics.

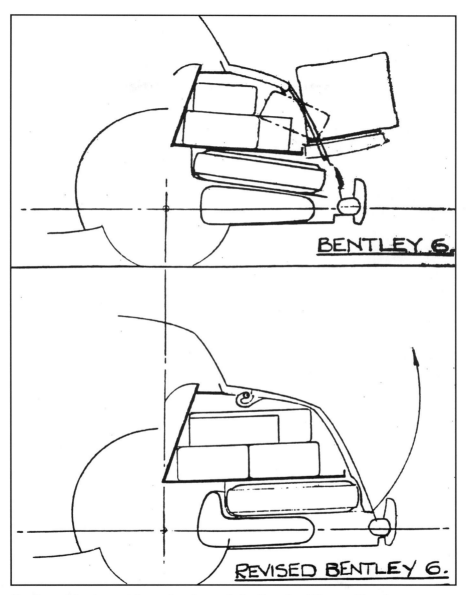

Outline of basic revisions that formed the Standard R-type Bentley.

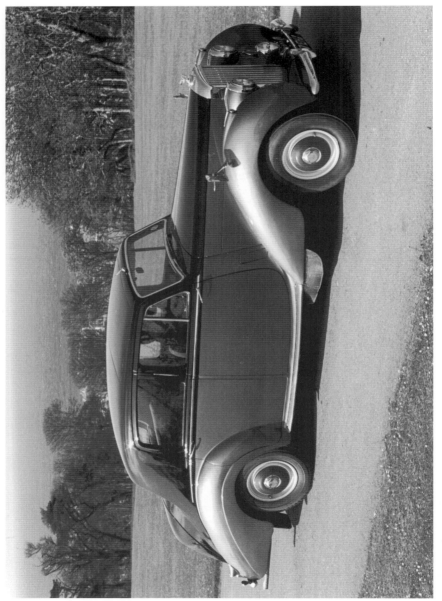

The standard Bentley R-type. A mature, reliable and durable car that proved popular at a crucial phase.

The Pininfarina Bentley Cresta outside the Farina works in 1948 before exhibiting at the Paris Salon.

A rear quarter view at the same location, where its elegance is portrayed.

CHAPTER EIGHT

The performance factor returns

The higher performance requirement of the late 1930s was aborted by the war's intervention and, as no Corniche model survived, this could have been disastrous for this sector of the model range plans. Additionally, its cause was not helped by the early post-war official attitudes, particularly towards the Company. Strangely these social attitudes did not pervade to the Continent and there was soon pressure again from *Sr* for more performance and different body styles to the more conservative offerings from Britain. The absence of a suitable experimental car did delay the Company's response to this particular request, although they were also preoccupied with the new skill requirements in body and trim, with developing the B-range engine and with early work on the next car. Nevertheless their limited response to *Sr* was to be key to the advent of their own proposal some time later, as is outlined below.

It is also clear that, similar to the enthusiasm for the 8-cylinder, the remaining 'old school' engineers still hankered after a more sporting Bentley. Such ideas were quietly pursued at Clan Foundry in support of *Sr* and, even when all car engineering transferred to Crewe in 1949, the idea survived albeit robustly driven by *Sr* himself. This was because Franco Britannique Automobiles had a requirement to compete with products from Peugeot and Talbot-Darracq. Early in 1948 a Mk VI chassis, modified in the area of the bulkhead, the rake angle of the steering column and the radiator to reduce bonnet height was taken to Farina in Tolino, Italy. This car is illustrated outside the Tolino factory prior to its being exhibited at the 1948 Paris Salon as the Bentley Cresta, with coachwork by Pininfarina. There was a further exhibit at the 1949 Salon and again in 1950 where it appeared in left-hand-drive form and with the front end styling revised back towards a somewhat more traditional treatment, but still a long way from the standard Bentley grill of the Mk VI. There were said to be some 17 of these cars built with bodies made under licence by Facel-Metallon and, at the time of writing, at least three survive including the first Facel-Metallon-bodied car B-447-CD shown here in recently first-class restored condition. The others are B-323-CD, being the earliest chassis, and seen at the Paris Salon in 1948 and B-476-DA which is left-hand-drive and fitted with a Pininfarina body which was at one time converted from right-hand to left- hand-drive and had its front end revised to the later style. More details of the history are shown with later matters in Appendix Two.

Subsequently, in January 1951, *Ev* produces an in-house 'futuristic proposal' based on the Bentley Cresta chassis, but he updated both the engine and transmission specifications. His affinity to matters previous is clear as the project is coded 'Corniche II'. His report states that the performance of the car must exceed that of previous Bentleys and must also exceed current competition from Healey at 114 mph and Aston-Martin at 117 mph. (Note:- This latter car was with W.O.Bentley's engine design which was taken over by David Brown Ltd when they bought Lagonda.) *Ev* sets a specification objective of 120 miles covered in the hour and a top speed of 125 mph. He concludes, with supporting calculations, that the Cresta chassis as supplied to France, fitted with the large-bore engine (3⅝-inches) and equipped with a [low drag] body built by H.J. Mulliner, using their light alloy construction, would meet this requirement. However, it was obvious that neither *Gry* nor *LS* were likely to be enthusiastic and he concludes with a telling comment, in my view, taking full account of the politics of the day at Crewe and I quote, "a very small amount of work would fall on the Design and Development Departments, since the chassis already exists. Messrs Mulliner are enthusiastic to proceed on the project". In my opinion, had this not been the case, the chance of production would have been remote and thus the importance of the Bentley Cresta chassis in enabling the return of the performance Bentley should be properly and fully recognised. Furthermore, *Ev* refers to the performance of the Bentley Cresta, as measured in December 1948. He notes that with the 4¼ litre engine delivering some 135 hp, the combination of a weight of 2 tons and a frontal area of 25.18 square feet, meant the maximum speed of Cresta was only 96.7 mph.

This was not on a par with that seen pre-war on either of the Paulin-designed bodies on B-27-LE nor 14-B-V. He then proposes a styling with a resulting frontal area more in line with the Paulin concept on B-27-LE and his styling drawing, dated September 1950, clearly shows its antecedence. He further defines the mechanical specification, with the return of the low-loss exhaust system as fitted to R.N.Dorey's *(Dor)* car absorbing only 6 hp but acceptable from the noise aspect for this project, and completes the specification with the fitment of a 3.42:1 axle and an overdrive gearbox (shades of Mk V) coupled to the 4½ litre engine. This, he estimates, will give 137 hp at the hubs as opposed to 135 hp gross from the 4¼ litre. He compares improvements in tyre resistance over pre-war technology and hence calculates that at 4400 rpm there will be enough power for a road speed of 128 mph, with the engine speed well below the critical speed of 5000 rpm. He concludes further that some road cars with heavier bodies and with a greater frontal area, as may be demanded by customers, may limit the speed to 116 mph and he recommends that for the production series, in order to give equivalent acceleration, that the use of a 3.72:1 axle would be preferred but he also recommends an external overdrive. After publication of the report a little more power was available from a modest increase in

The first Facel-Metallon body on B-447-CD – a recent photo after a complete restoration.

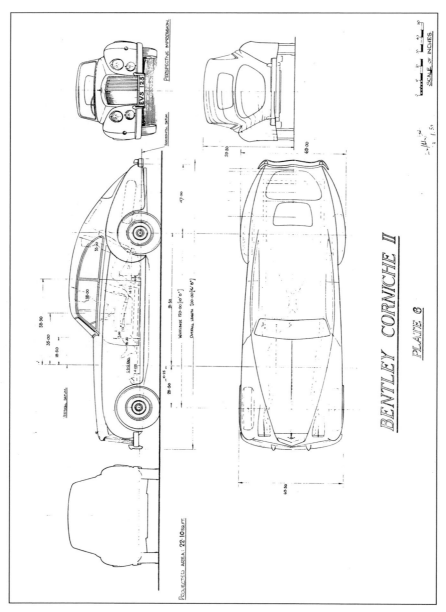

BENTLEY CORNICHE II

PLATE 6

Evernden's styling drawing where the form is taken from Georges Paulin's design for B-27-LE.

76

compression ratio resulting from the improvements in combustion chamber shape.

Happily, he was successful in persuading the powers that be and the result was the construction of 'Corniche II' on experimental chassis 9-B-VI registered as OLG 490 and known since as 'Olga'. She achieved 116 mph local to Crewe on her first test run, but was soon in France in the hands of *Sr* and a Crewe test driver. *Sr* must have been in his element when the car was exhibited at the Paris Salon in 1951 where an indicated 119 mph was seen on demonstration, but still recording over all the test work 18.1 mpg. In reality the car was somewhat over-geared for the power available and a direct-drive gearbox was fitted. This allowed 4500 rpm to be seen on the tachometer in top gear which equated to 124mph. Fuel consumption fell to an average 14.1 mpg during the ensuing hard driving test work. 'Olga' was handed to Sales Department in March 1952 with 11000 miles on the clock and eventually sold as chassis BC-26-A. Further developments took place on later cars and these are outlined in Appendix Two.

Thus the Bentley Continental Sports Saloon was announced and was road-tested and reported by Autocar in September 1953, where it was priced at £4980 without tax and said to be for export only. It could claim to be the most expensive but fastest four- to five-seat saloon in the world. There is no doubt that this model prolonged the life of the whole range, with Autocar speaking of driving it as 'another first' in motoring experience. It is plain that this model must rate as the ultimate accolade of the Rationalised Range concept although, but for the war's intervention, the Bentley V Corniche could have achieved this performance earlier, especially if the 8-cylinder model forecast for 1940 had been produced.

The prototype Bentley 'Corniche II', 9-B-VI, which succeeded in achieving its performance targets.

CHAPTER NINE

A short appraisal of the Rationalised Range

The foregoing completes, in somewhat abridged form, the story of the men, their actions and designs involved in a range of cars whose success was demonstrated by it resulting in the largest volume of cars produced in the Company's history until the R-type Bentley and the Rolls-Royce Silver Dawn ceased production in early 1955. The venerable Silver Wraith continued for some time further until the introduction of the new V-8 engine and production of the B-range engine for cars ceased. However, it was a range whose wider potential and appeal, for example in terms of performance, was to be seen inside the Company in 1939 or even slightly earlier, but was only publicly realised in 1952 with the advent of the Bentley Continental.

The full potential of the range, inclusive of the smaller models envisaged, was never to be realised but both in engineering and economic terms, all that *Hs*, *By* and indeed *Rm* foresaw was seen, but only in a limited way. It is to be measured not only by the market success of the standard model of the Bentley Mk VI, the Rolls-Royces Silver Wraith and Dawn but also by the fact that these practical products of the Rationalised Range returned the Chassis Division to profit throughout their production life.

Had it not been for the social upheavals of the war and the immediate post-war period, it is clear that the direction would have been very different to that eventually taken with the S-series, where high-performance models and indeed the use of the Bentley brand image gradually declined nearly to extinction until its revival in the mid-eighties with the advent of the fuel-injected Bentley Turbo R which, together with the later revival of the Continental, were responsible again for transforming the Company's image. Interestingly, the next time the theme of rationalisation was introduced was also in 1986 when, where appropriate, all parts were rationalised within the complete car range and some 2000 parts were removed from manufacture. The time of rationalisation had come again.

APPENDIX ONE

Modification data for Bentley cars 1946 to 1955.

Note that the following is taken from Service Bulletin BB.234 which states that in some cases a number of chassis were modified prior to those stated below and some were undoubtedly fitted to earlier cars in service. The chassis numbers quoted refer to the commencement of the continuous embodiment of these modifications on production.

Chassis Series	Description	Chassis Number
A	Servo damper	B-70-AK
	Squirt hole in connecting-rods	B-126-AK
	Shock absorber screwed inserts	B-250-AK
	Twin ignition coils / Parkerised tappets	B-1-AJ
	Hardened push-rods	B-31-AJ
	Modified horn push-button	B-185-AJ
B	AC Air Cleaner / SC carburettor needles Strengthened wheel disc flange	B-2-BH
	Heater return tap deleted / Heater drain tap added	B-70-BH
	Provision for 5-inch dynamo	B-122-BH
	Rocker cover breather	B-198-BH
	Modified interior door locks	B-228-BH
	Increased synchro cam angles	B-292-BH
	Modified distributor drive spring ring	B-398-BH
	Increased front shock absorber loading	B-185-BG
	Nebar rocker cover joint	B-303-BG
	Export body modifications	B-321-BG
C	Aluminium tappet doors / Larger rear hub bearings	B-2-CF
	Bronze exhaust valve guides	B-26-CF
	Modified clutch thrust race	B-164-CF
	Solid door striker plates	B-206-CF
	Horn supressor	B-218-CF
	Dunlop jacks	B-236-CF
	Wider opening radiator shutters	B-320-CF
	2.4-inch servo balance lever	B-344-CF
	5-inch dynamo	B-426-CF

	C&A cylinder head gasket /	
	Accelerator countershaft guard	B-1-CD
	13-degree brake expanders / 25-degree servo cams	B-17-CD
	Modified coolant pump	B-115-CD
	Improved rubber door seals /	
	Servo protection plate	B-347-CD
	Modified quicklift window stop	B-363-CD
	Extended petrol tank breather	B-475-CD
D	Low-lift camshaft / Lucas screen wipers /	
	modified core plugs	B-2-DA
	Oil caps in No.7 journal	B-62-DA
	Bench-type spring drive	B-128-DA
	Longer upper triangle levers	B-134-DA
	Short cylinder inserts	B-144-DA
	Rear shock damper linkage modification	B-200-DA
	Battery charging plug	B-252-DA
	Larger frontal area radiator /	
	Anti-spill valve in radiator	B-270-DA
	Chromium-plated servo plate	B-384-DA
	Strengthened door hinges	B-420-DA
	Increased diameter scuttle drain	B-492-DA
	$\frac{3}{8}$-inch cylinder studs	B-95-DZ
	N.S.front window winder	B-117-DZ
	Improved window channels	B-131-DZ
	Square-edge bearing, 1st- and 3rd-motion shafts	B-150-DZ
	Strengthened 3rd motion shaft splines	B-159-DZ
	8½-inch deflection front springs /	
	Radiator-heated demister /	
	Dip and switch headlamps	B-193-DZ
	Modified underseat heater /	
	Export features on all cars /	
	Fixed guide to front windows	B-237-DZ
	22½-degree servo cams, 3-inch balance levers	B-241-DZ
	Heater return tap re-introduced	B-273-DZ
	Revised inter-shoe brake linkage	B-493-DZ
E	Split-skirt pistons	B-2-EY
	Granodised piston rings	B-120-EY
	Portable hand inspection lamp	B-162-EY
	Luggage boot water trap	B-264-EY

	Progressive bump stops	B-466-EY
		(B-126-LEY)
	⅜-inch diameter rear axle bolts	B-1-EW
	Closer-fitting tappets	B-57-EW
	Graded pistons	B-111-EW
	Commonised dash	B-273-EW
	Forged rear spring shackle bracket	B-403-EW
F	Internal oil feed to distributor	B-2-FV
	Longer gear lever	B-138-FV
	Modified rear SD plates	B-444-FV
	Trico windscreen washer	B-1-FU
	Modified S.S. tube socket	B-244-FU
	Modified X.S. tube sockets	B-281-FU
G	Revised steering geometry /	
	Thicker-lipped brake drums / Anti-rumble brakes	B-1-GT
	2nd mod. to rear S.D. plates	B-67-GT
	Four foot mounted air cleaner	B-111-GT
	Improved rear number plate box /	
	Revised Bijur pipes to rear shackles	B-165-GT
	Reduced-speed fan	B-213-GT
	Keyhole sockets on gear control	B-281-LGT
	One-piece rear brake equi-lever	B-381-GT
H	Aluminium cam wheel / Electric clock /	
	Low-rate oil feed to clutch thrust /	
	11-inch clutch (light type) /	
	3-bush rear brake equi-support /	
	Modified starter solenoid switch	B-2-HR
	Lower bush R.S.D. link deleted	B-110-HR
	Speedo dip warning light	B-31-HP
	Large-bore carburettors /	
	Modified clutch spigot bearing	B-83-HP
	Closer-fitting 2nd- and 3rd-speed bushes	B-95-HP
	Triple pass de-mister inter. scheme	B-149-HP
	Longer bosses on R.S.D. plates	B-179-HP
J	Thicker R.S.D. plates	B-154-JO
	Modified water pump gland ring	B-61-JN

K	Triple by-pass R.H. de-mister (final)	B-2-KM
	Modified ammeter	B-64-KM
	New-type ignition condenser	B-117-KL
L	Steel oil caps in crankshaft	B-40-LJ
	Oil feed adaptor air bottle	B-170-LJ
	11-inch heavy duty clutch	B-300-LJ
M	3⅝-inch-bore engine / Thickened crankshaft webs / Full-Flow oil filter / Twin exhaust system (RH cars only)	B-2-MD
	Side scuttle ventilators	B-29-MB
	Insulated dynamo	B-313-MB
N	Increased front damping	B-210-NZ
	Twin condensors	B-292-NZ
	SP carburettor needles (R.H. cars only)	B-478-NZ
	Short dwell detent on 1st-gear selector	B-500-NZ / B-360-LNZ
	Repositioned oil gauge connection on crankcase	B-123-NY
	Mk II headlamp	B-169-NY
	Stiffened clutch casing	B-253-NY
	3-position heater and demister switches / 120-degree opening ventilator windows / Rear window de-mister	B-311-NY
P	Reversion to old-yype front wheel studs	B-22-PV
	Solid pins and shield on servo	B-284-PV
	Hot and cold de-mister	B-53-PU
	Exhaust heat shields	B-159-PU
	Needle rollers in clutch release levers	B-185-PU
	Reduced friction on steering connections	B-215-PU
R	Revised luggage boot / Automatic SU carburettors / Revised attitude rear springs / Revised rear shock damper springs / two-speed windscreen wiper / Pop-out cigar lighter / Separately-housed main fuse / Castor angle wedges	B-2-RT
	Corrugated bottom water hose	B-68-RT

S	Taper roller bearings on rear axle pinion (except 12:41 axle)	B-380-SR
	3½-second slow leak on front dampers	B-61-SP
	Parco lubrized tappets	B-425-SP
	Taper roller bearings on pinion gear 12:41 Axle	B-433-SP
T	6.75 compression ratio cylinder head	B-93-TO
	Deletion of non-opposed springs in side steering tube	B-313-TO
	All-welded frames	B-349-TO
	Metal facia / Cable-operated hot and cold de-mister and underseat heater	B-2-TN
	Hard clay gasket	B-372-TN
	Deletion of reduced friction mod. on steering connections	B-390-TN
	Revised throttle controls for synchromesh gearbox	B-436-TN
U	Aluminium flywheel housing	B-35-UL
	Improved-type underseat tool tray	B-66-UM
	Introduction of B-VI -type tie rod	B-212-UM
W	Flywheel inertia ring on cars with auto gearbox	B-236-WH
	Dynamo-type mounting strap on starter motor	B-270-WH
	Thicker 3rd-motion shaft thrust washer	B-89-WG
	Compensator pipe between front and rear servo (automatic)	B-183-WG
X	Strengthened jaws on front brake operating links	B-60-XF
Y	12:41 rear axle (all cars)	B-1-YA
	Elimination of chromium-plated servo pressure plate	B-123-YD
	Long stroke starter pinion	B-138-YD
	Flexibox seal on water pump	B-160-YD
	Bentley Continental-type de-misting	B-246-YD
Z	Improved cold-starting device	B-1-ZX
	2nd-speed start	B-73-ZX
	Ferodo washers and drain slots to crankshaft vibration damper	B-212-ZY

Bentley Continental

A	Reduced-compression-height pistons	BC-19-A
C	Commonised cylinder head	BC-4-C
	Deletion of non-opposed springs in steering side tube	BC-18-C
	All-welded frame	BC-21-C
	Deletion of reduced friction mod. on steering connections	BC-30-C
	Introduction of Bentley Mk VI-type gearbox tie-rod	BC-50-C
	Flywheel inertia rings on cars fitted with auto-gearbox	BC-70-C
	Thicker third-motion shaft thrust washer	BC-78-C
D	3¾-inch-bore engine / Compensator pipe between front and rear servo (auto)	BC-1-D
	Strengthened jaws on front brake operating links	BC-5-D
	Elimination of chromium-plated servo pressure plate	BC-12-D
	Flexibox seal in water pump	BC-35-D
	Long-stroke starter pinion	BC-37-D
	Improved cold-starting device	BC-43-D
	2nd-speed start	BC-47-D

B-323-CD. Daninos's car ordered on Farina, Tolino, Italy and photographed outside the works in 1948.

APPENDIX TWO

More on the antecedents to the Bentley Continental cars

The Bentley Cresta

The development of this variant of the standard Mk VI chassis resulted from pressure from the Continent in the immediate postwar period where independent Continental coachbuilders were anxious to resume business, short of chassis and hence anxious to buy high-class British chassis. Naturally, even in the United Kingdom, production did not meet demand but there was active encouragement, through the taxation regimes, to export. Coachbuilders in Switzerland such as Graber and Franay in France were in the forefront of demand but the market requirement was also for a more *avant garde* approach to styling than that suited to the demand of the more traditional British clientel and provided by the English coachbuilders that re-entered the market after the war. The Bentley Mk VI chassis, as built to match the standard steel body, which was supplied for the majority of production chassis, resulted in too high a bonnet line and too upright a column position to achieve the lower profiles regarded as 'a point' for Continental tastes.

By 1947 *Sr* was demanding not only a left-hand-drive version of the standard car but also, for coachbuilt chassis, modifications to lower the column and the bonnet line. Such an approach was anathema to the concept of rationalised production but nevertheless, in support of the need to export, the Company was prepared to respond. The focus of this demand came from a co-operation between *Sr* and the owner of Forges et Ateliers de Construction d'Eure et Loir (FACEL), Monsieur Jean Daninos, whose company built bodies for the French volume car makers such as Panhard. It is not clear who was the driving force behind the requirement but it is true that *Sr* and Jean Daninos were much more than seller and buyer. The first chassis to feature a lowered column and reduced bonnet/radiator height was B-323-CD, ordered on the factory by Franco Britannique Automobiles and which was ex-works on 13. April 1948 and shipped to France on the 30th. The inter-departmental memos that described and acceded to the request cannot now be traced, but it was this chassis that was the foundation of the later evolutions. B-323-CD was and remains a right-hand-drive car and still exists, although not apparently in good order, within the Mahy Collection in Belgium. Daninos originally ordered the body for B-323-CD from Farina in Tolino Italy. The car was exhibited at the Paris Salon in 1948 and further photographs are shown in this appendix. Note the wide radiator grill which was not liked by the Company and the subsequent cars were to incorporate a revised narrower radiator grill as shown on B-447-CD.

In a letter to Stanley Sedgwick, Daninos records that the first car was subsequently modified by FACEL to the same style as the later cars which explains why the car currently sports a double 'ff' badge signifying that it was a FACEL car. It originally bore a badge showing a single 'f' denoting design and manufacture by Farina. B-447-CD is the first complete car built under an agreement between Farina and FACEL and this car is also depicted in the photographs and, at the time of writing, is the only known survivor built completely by FACEL. Daninos recalls that he built some seventeen Crestas but the Company records, having been researched extensively, put this figure at eleven. It is also clear that the specification evolved to further lower the bonnet line, which meant a complete revision to the engine air cleaner and further repositioning of underbonnet equipment. Records also show the introduction of a lowered bonnet and steering column to the left-hand-drive specification, the first chassis being B-476-DA completed at Crewe as a right-hand-drive chassis and shipped to Clan Foundry for conversion and specification by Engineering Department prior to being shipped in November 1948. The chassis was shipped to Farina for bodying and this car also still exists and is at the time of writing nearing completion of a full restoration.

Following this chassis, there were at least three derivatives of the Cresta chassis supplied exclusively to Franco Britannique Automobiles for bodying by FACEL. These were known as Cresta I (B-323-CD), II, III and IV although the differences between III and IV appear minimal. Cresta production ran until about 1950 when it was clear that the Company had ideas of its own. Whilst the number of Cresta cars that were delivered remains unclear when viewed against the seventeen declared, from memory, by M. Daninos, those that are confirmed are to be seen in the table presented. The only known survivors at the time of writing are B-323-CD, B-447-CD, B-167-JN and B-476-DA being two by Farina and two by FACEL. It is also known that B-99-LEW was scrapped in Egypt, but the fate of the rest is unknown.

Returning to events at the Company, a few members of Engineering were intent on producing a high-performance variant based on the 4½ litre Mk VI around the end of 1950. Various authors of Bentley publications contend that the Cresta body is the forerunner of the Bentley Continental but this is actually not the case, although Cresta IV, as a chassis specification, was the actual specification of the Bentley Continental when fitted with the 4½ litre B60 engine for production. Curiously the last car of the Cresta chassis series, purchased by Daninos himself, was B-98-KM which was completed in early 1951 and, whilst not exactly of the Cresta body design, as illustrated, the car was returned to the UK in July 1951 and was fitted with the 4½ litre engine

B-447-CD. The first Facel bodied-car under the licence arrangement with Farina. The photograph is of the car as she was in 1996.

B-476-DA. The first left-hand-drive chassis with Cresta revisions bodied by Farina.

B-98-KM. The last Cresta delivered to Franco Britannique Automobiles and retrospectively fitted with stiffer front springs and a 4½ litre engine.

at about the same time that the prototype 9-B-VI (Olga) was completed. Daninos claims his car was a 120 mph car. B-98-KM also still exists and was seen receiving attention during 1995 at the workshops of P & A Woods.

Origins of the Bentley Continental body scheme.

In January 1951 *Ev* issued a report entitled 'Corniche II – A New Record-Breaking Saloon Sports Car' which outlines the project and provides supporting calculations that determine the specification both of the prototype, for a record attempt, and the production version. *Ev* clearly outlines the project's antecedants being a combination of "The Cresta chassis fitted with the increased capacity engine" and a lightweight body styled and outlined by *Ev* but constructed by H.J. Mulliner using their lightweight construction methods already in production. It is the evolution of *Ev*'s styling thoughts that demonstrate how the Corniche II owes the majority of its design to the Embiricos car by Paulin more than to the design of the Cresta, although there is some obvious synergy between the two. The body by Farina and subsequently FACEL did have one advantage over that of Paulin in that it had a lower drag coefficient at 0.397 as opposed to that determined by wind tunnel tests on the Paulin design which measured 0.473. The major improvement of some 17% was more than offset by a 19.5% larger frontal area than Paulin's design, particularly when coupled with a weight 2.06 tons which was heavier than the standard car! He records his view that "the style of the Cresta I is totally unsuitable for this [project]". However, whilst his report comments that "the layout is generally similar to Embiricos and the frontal area is almost the same (22.10 sq.ft.) the drag coefficient will approximate more nearly to that of Cresta I".

He achieved the reduced coefficient by fairing the front wings into the body and with other detail changes. His judgement was obviously sound as events show that the car, 9-B-VI, in production form with a direct-drive gearbox and a 12:41 ratio achieved its maximum design speed target. However, performance of each individual car was seen to be greatly influenced by the choice of road tyres which had very different loss factors. (The lower the power absorption, the lower the life of the tread.) Details of the overall chassis specification are well known, but I repeat that if the design modifications, initiated by *Sr* and Daninos, had not been introduced, the 'politics' of the day would have put the whole idea at high risk as there was considerable anxiety about determining the form of the successor to the Mk VI and therefore there was a severe limitation on Engineering resources available. Interestingly *Ev* makes comment on the lack of need for Engineering design support on two occasions in his report.

Thus the importance of Paulin's work on the ultimate success of the

D8 120. Delage whose body design by Paulin predates the Embiricos Bentley, B-27-LE.

rationalised range is clearly key, but his body style, as built on the Embiricos Bentley B-27-LE, was preceded by one fitted to a D8 120 Delage which, as shown in the photograph, is similarly styled although it retains its production-style radiator and the rear wing treatment is different and probably less aerodynamic. *AHB* recalls being with Paulin in Paris in 1939 and seeing the Delage en route. Paulin commented that the performance of the design had not been all he had wished and it was for this reason that the classic Bentley radiator was removed, with no quarter given to compromise.

The Delage car also survives, being found ripe for restoration in 1995 in Bordeaux. It is to be hoped it receives the attention it deserves. Photographs of the car have previously been published in Tout L'histoire Delage by Alain Dollfus. I am grateful for this information to both *AHB* and to the Secretary and Registrar of the Delage Section of the Vintage Sports Car Club, VSCC.

Notes on the evolution of the Bentley Continental Design

The Bentley Continental chassis had few modifications that were not featured on standard R-type chassis as is clearly seen from the modifications shown in Appendix 1, with the notable exception of the 3¾-inches-bore engine to further enhance acceleration. The early 4.9-litre engines did not feature some of the later modifications adopted during the S-series production,but followed the then standard design. The increase in bore size was achieved by boring out the cylinder block but fitting an high phosphorous iron liner in combination with chrome plated top compression ring, which proved to give excellent bore wear and reduced the running-in regimes and problems encountered. This package thus became the overhaul standard for all the B60 engines in service. The advent of the Continental car also brought about the demise of the column gearchange for left-hand-drive cars and this was replaced by a centre gearchange assembly, but still utilising the lever gate mounted in the traditional position on the right hand side of the chassis.

All coachbuilders were able to take the Continental chassis and thus not all cars are to the H.J. Mulliner fastback design now known as the H.J. Mulliner R-type Continental.The survival rate of these Continental cars is higher than the average for the whole series, which is a measure of their long-term appeal.

All the Bentley Crestas

Chassis Number	Chassis Shipped	Guarantee Date	Body	1st Owner	Current Owner
B-323-CD	30.4.48	15.10.48	f/ff	J. Daninos	Mahy Collection
B-447-CD	2.7.48	23.10.48	ff	M.A. Matos	John Donner
B-476-DA (L) Converted at Clan Foundry	25.11.48	28.12.49	f	Precisa Seattle	HJT Channing
B-402-LEY	15.6.49	24.11.49	ff	K. Abildgaard	Unknown
B-99-LEW	16. 6.49	19.9.50	ff	S.Circurel	Scrapped in Egypt
B-441-LEW	29.10.49	29 5.50	ff	S.A.S. Prince Rainier	Unknown
B-443-LEW	29.10.49	15.11.50	ff	F.L.Dreyfus	Unknown
B-445-LEW	22.12.49	20.1.51	ff	Marquis de Albano Dr Nunriante	Unknown
B-541-FU	7.4 50	6.9.50	ff	J.J.Setton	Unknown
B-167-JN	22.2.51	22.2.51	ff	F.Lugeon	Unknown (in France)
B-98-KM	8.1.51 (18.7.51)	16.10.51	ff*	J. Daninos	H.G.Bullen

*Although a Cresta chassis, later modified to take 4½ litre engine, not a Cresta body but a Coupe. Not included by Mr. Daninos as part of the seventeen that he recalls producing.

**B-141-GT is also thought to be a Cresta but the records are missing. Details are:-

B-141-GT	14.6.50	26.10.50	ff ?	A.Dardari	Unknown

Acknowledgement

The author wishes to thank both Rolls-Royce plc. and Rolls-Royce Motor Cars Ltd. for permission to publish this book. I would also express my appreciation to the Rolls-Royce Heritage Trust in whose name this book is published and for the Trust's encouragement.

I also acknowledge the considerable help gven by the Bentley Drivers Club (BDC) and the Rolls-Royce Enthusiasts' Club (RREC) and I thank them for their contribution and support. In particular, I would like to express my appreciation for all the help personally provided by Peter Baines (RREC), Bill Port (BDC) Ian Rimmer (Rolls-Royce Motor Car Ltd) Mike Evans (Rolls-Royce and the Rolls-Royce Heritage Trust) and last but not least my good friend Alec Harvey-Bailey for his apposite recollections and his invaluable anecdotes. Without this support it would have been an impossible task to give both the lecture at the 50th. Anniversary Celebrations for the first cars from the Crewe factory held in Buxton in April 1996 and to publish this book.

INDEX

Companies

Illustrations

Personalities

Rolls-Royce:
  Colonel Barrington *(Bn)*   29
  Ray Dorey *(Dor)*   74
  A G Elliott *(E)*   20, 27
  H I F Evernden *(Ev)*   41, 49, 65,
    66, 73, 74, 94
  Harry Grylls *(Gry)*   53, 65, 74
  Alec Harvey-Bailey *(AHB)*   9,
    29, 96
  R W Harvey-Bailey *(By)*   20, 23,
    27, 41, 43, 49, 51, 79
  E W Hives *(Hs)*   20, 23, 27, 49,
    51, 54, 58, 79
  Claude Johnson *(CJ)*   9
  F Llewellyn-Smith *(LS)*   65, 74
  W A Robotham *(Rm)*   23, 32, 37,
    41, 43, 49, 53, 65, 79
  Charles Rolls *(CSR)*   8
  Sir Henry Royce *(R)*   9, 20, 29
  Walter Sleator *(Sr)*   41, 73, 77,
    89, 94

Others:
  W O Bentley   29, 41, 74
  M. Jean Daninos   89, 90, 94
  George Eyston   41
  Eddie Hall   41
  Air Marshal 'Bomber' Harris   36
  HRH Princess Elizabeth   13
  Georges Paulin   41, 74, 94, 96
  Pininfarina   73
  Stanley Sedgewick   90

Miscellaneous

B-range engines   23, 28, 29, 54,
  61, 79
  B60   29, 61, 65
  B80   32
Brooklands   41, 43
Clan Foundry   51, 53, 73, 90
C-range oil engines   51
Crewe factory   10, 54, 58, 73, 74
Delage D8 120   96
Monthlery   41

The Historical Series is published as a joint initiative by the Rolls-Royce Heritage Trust and The Sir Henry Royce Memorial Foundation.

Also published in the series:
No.1 Rolls-Royce – the formative years 1906-1939
    Alec Harvey-Bailey RRHT 2nd edition 1983
No.2 The Merlin in perspective – the combat years
    Alec Harvey-Bailey, RRHT 4th edition 1995
No.3 Rolls-Royce – the pursuit of excellence
    Alec Harvey-Bailey and Mike Evans, HRMF 1984
No.4 In the beginning – the Manchester origins of Rolls-Royce
    Mike Evans, RRHT 1984
No.5 Rolls-Royce – the Derby Bentleys
    Alec Harvey-Bailey, HRMF 1985
No.6 The early days of Rolls-Royce – and the Montagu family
    Lord Montagu of Beaulieu, RRHT 1986
No.7 Rolls-Royce – Hives, the quiet tiger
    Alec Harvey-Bailey, HRMF 1985
No.8 Rolls-Royce – Twenty to Wraith
    Alec Harvey-Bailey,HRMF 1986
No.9 Rolls-Royce and the Mustang
    David Birch, RRHT 1987
No.10 From Gipsy to Gem with diversions, 1926-1986
    Peter Stokes, RRHT 1987
No.11 Armstrong Siddeley – the Parkside story, 1896-1939
    Ray Cook, RRHT 1989
No.12 Henry Royce – mechanic
    Donald Bastow, RRHT 1989
No.14 Rolls-Royce – the sons of Martha
    Alec Harvey-Bailey, HRMF 1989
No.15 Olympus – the first forty years
    Alan Baxter, RRHT 1990
No.16 Rolls-Royce piston aero engines – a designer remembers
    A A Rubbra, RRHT 1990
No.17 Charlie Rolls – pioneer aviator
    Gordon Bruce, RRHT 1990
No.18 The Rolls-Royce Dart – pioneering turboprop
    Roy Heathcote, RRHT 1992
No.19 The Merlin 100 series – the ultimate military development
    Alec Harvey-Bailey and Dave Piggott, RRHT 1993
No.20 Rolls-Royce – Hives' turbulent barons
    Alec Harvey-Bailey, HRMF 1992
No.21 Rolls-Royce – The Crecy Engine
    Nahum, Foster-Pegg, Birch, RRHT 1994
No.22 Vikings at Waterloo – the wartime work on the Whittle jet engine by the
    Rover Company
    David S Brooks, RRHT 1997

Books are available from:
Rolls-Royce Heritage Trust, Rolls-Royce plc, Moor Lane, PO Box 31, Derby DE24 8BJ

ROLLS-ROYCE

HERITAGE TRUST